T0090491

BLACK DIAMOND - BLACK GOLD

THE DANVILLE LADY TOMAHAWKS

PHYLLIS ADKISSON-SMITH

WESTBOW
PRESS®
A DIVISION OF THOMAS NELSON
& ZONDERVAN

Copyright © 2023 Phyllis Adkisson-Smith.

All rights reserved. No part of this book may be used or reproduced by any means, graphic, electronic, or mechanical, including photocopying, recording, taping or by any information storage retrieval system without the written permission of the author except in the case of brief quotations embodied in critical articles and reviews.

WestBow Press books may be ordered through booksellers or by contacting:

WestBow Press
A Division of Thomas Nelson & Zondervan
1663 Liberty Drive
Bloomington, IN 47403
www.westbowpress.com
844-714-3454

Because of the dynamic nature of the Internet, any web addresses or links contained in this book may have changed since publication and may no longer be valid. The views expressed in this work are solely those of the author and do not necessarily reflect the views of the publisher, and the publisher hereby disclaims any responsibility for them.

Any people depicted in stock imagery provided by Getty Images are models, and such images are being used for illustrative purposes only. Certain stock imagery © Getty Images.

Scripture quotations are taken from the Holy Bible, New International Version®, NIV®. Copyright © 1973, 1978, 1984 by Biblica, Inc.™ Used by permission of Zondervan. All rights reserved worldwide.

ISBN: 979-8-3850-0269-6 (sc)
ISBN: 979-8-3850-0268-9 (e)

Library of Congress Control Number: 2023913025

Print information available on the last page.

WestBow Press rev. date: 9/26/2023

Wilbur "Yank" Adkisson

The Danville Lady Tomahawks

CONTENTS

1 The Beginning of the End   1

2 Black Diamond - Black Gold
The Danville Lady Tomahawks   4

3 Veterans Administration   5

    Misdiagnosis: A Long Road Home   6

4 The Lady Tomahawks   7

5 Yank Saw an Opportunity: His Big
Intervention   12

6 Black Gold: The Lady Tomahawks   14

7 Softball Season   16

8 From Fast-Pitch to Slow-Pitch   21

9 Playing Against the Umpires and
Officials   23

    Disrespectful Spectators   24

    Integration   25

10 Getting Started   27

    Pitching Intimidation   28

    Development of a Young Team   29

11 The Adkisson Family   31

12 Are You Your Brother's Keeper?   33

13 Life after the War   35

Opportunity Only Knocks Once   40

14 Moving On with Life   42

15 The Woman Who Stood Beside the Man   44

16 Interesting Facts   46

17 The Tomahawks Roll Call and That Little Brown Bat   50

18 Beautiful Memories By The Lady Tomahawks!   52

19 The Danville Philly League All-Star Team   65

20 Great-Granddaughter's Dedication: Ciara Smith   67

21 Royal Thrill Article   68

22 Group Wants to Rename Park   69

23 Big Yank's Sayings   70

24 The Lady Tomahawk Game Song   71

25 Home Field   72

Danville City Parks Played In   73

26 Uniform Colors   74

27 Three Original Tomahawks   75

28 Places Played   76

29 Played Under Other Sponsors   77

30 Rival Teams in the Danville Philly
League   78

31 Certificate Amateur Softball
Association   79

32 Tomahawks Team Captains   80

33 The Tomahawks Bat Boy(s) and
Bat Girl(s)   81

34 Tomahawks Coaching Staff   82

35 Honorable Mention   83

36 All-Star Softball Team   84

37 Deceased Tomahawks   85

38 Deceased Tomahawks Coaches   86

39 Special Recognition   87

40 Facts   88

41 Dedication   91

THE BEGINNING OF THE END

On May 4, 1998, I received a disturbing phone call from my mother. Her call left me shaken and physically ill. My mother broke the news to me that my father had been in a car accident. She asked me if I could come home to help her.

"Of course, I can, and I will be there as soon as I can book a flight," I replied. I knew she needed help.

The paramedics examined my father and released him into my mother's care to take him home. They told her he was just fine, and he should be his old self in a few days. Mom was physically shaken. She was not in a good place emotionally. Mom requested that all of us children come home to give additional support in taking care of our dad.

As soon as my younger brother and sister received the call, they dropped what they were doing and rushed to Illinois to help comfort our mother and to make sure our father was all right. Both of my siblings lived in Indiana.

My sister arrived in Illinois before my younger brother. She did not like the way my father responded. He was acting confused, talking slowly, having a difficult time getting his thoughts together, and drooling around the mouth. She immediately took Dad back to the hospital. He was seen again in the emergency room. The doctor told him he had high blood pressure, and his potassium level was low. After this evaluation, he was given additional medication and sent home.

Upon my brother's arrival, he immediately knew our father wasn't acting like his normal self. My brother picked up the phone and called me. He began to explain that our father didn't look well, and he was acting strangely. I asked him if he could describe his physical appearance and to ask him a few questions to get an appropriate response. As my brother was asking questions and examining him, he quickly realized that our father wasn't that quick-witted man anymore. He also observed our father had difficulty answering basic questions.

As my brother was describing his observation to me, we simultaneously said, "He had a stroke!"

At that moment, my brother and I realized we needed to act fast and get my father to the veterans' hospital.

BLACK DIAMOND -
BLACK GOLD
THE DANVILLE LADY
TOMAHAWKS

Phyllis Adkisson-Smith

VETERANS ADMINISTRATION

The stroke left the left side of my father's body paralyzed. By the time he arrived at the hospital, he had a hard time following commands and had slurred speech. The veterans' hospital doctor admitted him to neurology for twenty-three hours of observation, then full admission. He was eventually transferred to a rehabilitation medicine service. After his brief stay at the hospital, my mother had him transferred to a different facility.

My mother took him to the Rehabilitation Center of Urbana, Illinois, to receive adequate care. Our hope was for him to regain mobility.

MISDIAGNOSIS:
A LONG ROAD HOME

After listening to the specialist at the rehabilitation center, I knew my father's recovery was going to be a long and slow process. Time was not on our side. My siblings and I tried to be optimistic and looked forward to a speedy recovery. We knew valuable time had been lost when he was misdiagnosed.

As my father lay there in that lonely hospital bed, I knew he would no longer be the vibrant man to whom I'd always looked for advice, guidance, and wisdom. He would not be able to protect and provide for my mother. I also knew he would not be able to coach the game that he so deeply cared for and loved. He would not be able to carry the torch that had shined so brightly for the Danville Lady Tomahawks. It was absolutely the beginning of the end.

THE LADY TOMAHAWKS
OF
DANVILLE, ILLINOIS

(BLACK DIAMOND - BLACK GOLD)

The Danville Lady Tomahawks were one of the first African American ladies' fast-pitch softball teams in Illinois. Wilbur Adkisson, also known as "Yank," was the founder and manager of the Danville Lady Tomahawks. The team was organized in May 1960 at Lincoln Park.

Yank was an ex-professional Negro league baseball player who saw a need in the African American community to help African American females through sports. He became an assistant coach for Jewel "Jake" Butler. Jake was African American, and his team was composed of African American young ladies, who had already established the Lincoln Park UAW–CIO 579 Whippets softball team.

Yank had coached the previous year with Jake. Jake and Yank had several things in common. They were friends and from the same neighborhood. They both worked at General Motors, loved the game of baseball/softball, and wanted to give back to their community. They shared the same vision of giving the young ladies in the community something tangible to do.

Yank and Jake talked often about Yank's dream of starting his own softball team. Yank thought it would be a good idea to observe Jake and learn how the women's softball league was organized and run. He would also become familiar with the rules of the AAU (Amateur Athletic Union), what uniforms the young ladies could wear, and how the Danville Philly League worked. The Danville Philly League was a city parks and recreation softball league and only played softball during the summer season.

This was new and unfamiliar territory for Yank. He played baseball and never had a reason to learn the finer details of organizing his own team. He was excited to take part in this new adventure. After all, he loved being around children and helping young people wherever and whenever he possibly could. This was one of his valuable attributes.

Jake was starting a new season. He had approximately seventy-five young ladies try out for his Lincoln Park team. Jake chose twenty-five young ladies. Unfortunately, he could only carry twenty-five on his roster into the Danville Philly League.

On that warm summer day, he had to send fifty young ladies home. The young ladies were heartbroken. Yank could not let this happen. He saw an opportunity to save broken hearts and start his own team. He had no idea that starting his own team was going to happen sooner than he had anticipated. He knew that he could not let those girls walk away from the game. Yank had to act immediately.

Yank asked Jake if he had chosen all the girls that he wanted. Jake replied, "Yes!" Yank asked the same question again. Jake looked down at his list of names, looked at the girls he had chosen, and replied to Yank with a heartfelt but firm, *"Yes!"*

Yank said to Jake, "If you have chosen your team, then I will take the rest of the young ladies." **We talked about me starting my own team in the future. I guess today is that day!"**

Jake gave Yank his blessing. Jake hated losing a knowledgeable coach, but he wanted Yank to fulfill his dream of coaching his own team. Jake recognized Yank's passion and love for the game, and he did not want to hold him back.

Yank sprang into action. He yelled, "If you want to play softball, then go down under the big acorn tree in *right* field and wait for me there!"

Over the years, Yank and Jake formed a solid bond through supporting girls' and women's sports.

The Tomahawks were like black gold to my father. He referred to them as black gold, playing on a black diamond. The infield is in the shape of a diamond and his infield players were predominantly black. Therefore, he called it the black diamond. The Lady Tomahawk players were pure gold to him and the African American community.

Mrs. Phyllis Adkisson-Smith, Mr. Wilbur "Yank" Adkisson, Mr. Jewel "Jake" Butler

Yank and Jake remained friends until Jake's death in 1974.

YANK SAW AN OPPORTUNITY: HIS BIG INTERVENTION

With that in mind, the utmost and greatest Lady Tomahawk team was assembled in Danville, Illinois.

Year after year, the Lady Tomahawks gave the African American community a sense of pride and cohesiveness, a bond that has not been seen in the community since Yank's stroke (May 1998). The team encouraged and motivated young ladies to focus their energy and time on the black diamond. The Tomahawks carried their high morals and pride of Danville, Illinois with them throughout central Illinois and into the neighboring states of Tennessee and Indiana.

These young ladies were disciplined, on the field and off. The Lady Tomahawks carried their self-confidence, respect, and discipline into their everyday lives. When you looked at them, you saw ladies who became educators, administrators, social workers, homemakers, nurses, and workers in the church. Some of them became prominent leaders within the Black community.

Yank spent the better half of his life on the George Carver Park softball field trying to make life better for each young lady who stepped on that field. In 1998, Yank was in a car accident, and he was no longer able to coach. He could no longer carry the torch for the Lady Tomahawks. Yank passed away in 2002.

Today, Yank's dream for the Danville youth lives on through various community programs.

BLACK GOLD: THE LADY TOMAHAWKS

The Lady Tomahawks were one of the best teams ever established in Illinois. The team was made up of young girls in the African American community. Their ages ranged from nine to occasionally twenty-five or older.

Our team, the Lady Tomahawks, was an elite group of athletes. They were trained by Yank and his coaching staff in the summer months from May through July. We played in tournaments during August and September. Our home field was located at George Carver Park.

Carver Park is located between Seminary and Williams Streets. Both streets are major roads that run east and west through the heart of the city. They were the lifeline of the Black community. These streets were heavily traveled by the citizens of Danville, Illinois. The physical address is 420 E. Williams Street. The softball field was named Carver Park. It shared the name of the park located on the north side of the street. Consequently, in the year 2000, the name was changed to Adkisson's Field in honor of my father, Yank, for his contribution and dedication to female sports.

The Lady Tomahawks were a loyal group of young ladies. We were the pride and joy of the African American community. We practiced hard and played even harder in our softball games. Losing games was not in our vocabulary. To lose a game was a loss for our community. As young ladies, we were proud of our success and were highly respected by our fans.

SOFTBALL SEASON

We could not wait for spring to arrive in the Midwest. After a rough, dark, cold winter, spring was a long-awaited and welcome sight. It was the green light for softball season to start. Softball was our life. We loved playing the game! People would find the young ladies at practice from Monday through Friday from 5:30 in the evening until 8:00 or 9:00 at night. The park was equipped with lights that allowed the girls to practice late. The city did not provide the park with practice lights, bases, dugouts, or a water fountain. Yank had to petition the city's parks and recreation department several times to make the park equal to the other city parks.

Saturdays were usually reserved for games or good, rigid practice. Sometimes we would play a pickup game with the men in the community. Most of the time, the men would lose. Occasionally, the Lady Tomahawks would play games on Sundays. The girls preferred not to play games on Sundays. Sundays were reserved in most households for church fellowship, family gatherings, and relaxation. However, we would always play on Memorial Day and the Fourth of July. Many of the parents complained because they loved celebrating the holidays with family, friends, and barbecue cookouts. Nevertheless, most of the parents and friends came out to support the team. People held their cookouts after the game. It seemed as if the whole African American community was there supporting the team, win or lose.

The Tomahawks began to play together at a young age and continued to play together into adulthood. Yank put together a team of girls who showed potential and who were enthusiastic athletes. These players were the heart and soul of the team. They were his starting team (the Danville Lady Tomahawks).

The Tomahawks taught us how to be leaders in the Danville community.

RED-White-Blue Uniform with Yank and Mr. Williams

In the Philly League, you could not play until you were twelve years old. Yank had a group of younger girls who ranged in age from approximately nine to fifteen. Yank changed the game by creating a younger team of girls. These girls would observe the veteran players and play with them during practice. He called these young ladies his "farm team." These young ladies worked very hard cultivating their skills. They had to learn to play every position on the field. Base running, stealing bases, sliding, and bunting became second nature to them. It was a pleasure watching the enthusiasm and the willingness to become a Tomahawk player.

Yank would mold them into the positions where they showed the most potential. Some of the players were very versatile and could play and master different positions.

Yank's motto was, "Everyone should be able to play." With that said, Yank and his seasoned players would encourage the younger girls to practice hard and not be discouraged. Sitting on the bench game after game was very uncomfortable and disappointing to the younger players." As rookie players, they could not wait to get off that bench! They loved the game and were eager to play.

Yank would encourage the younger girls by saying, "Pay attention and learn the game." It was not long before Yank's wisdom and leadership paid off for his young team. In 1990, the Junior Tomahawks became city champions.

Douglas I champs

Commercial-News photo by Phil Stauder

Members of the East Central Illinois Tomahawks are: (back row from left) Yvonne Summers, Melissa Stone, Wilbur Adkisson, Evonda Goings, Linda Cooper; (front from left) Debra Robinson, P.J. Cunningham, Lisa Dye, batgirl Faye Kirk, Brenda Morris and Gayle Brandon.

Champs

FROM FAST-PITCH TO SLOW-PITCH

The Lady Tomahawks started off as a fast-pitch team and became a slow-pitch team in the summer of 1976. We would play a fast-pitch game one day and the next day a slow-pitch game. On several occasions, we would play a fast-pitch game on Saturday morning and a slow-pitch game Saturday evening. The first two innings were very funny. Our team had to adjust to the slow-pitched ball. We were striking out left and right. However, once everyone adjusted, it was all over for the opposing team.

We, the Tomahawks, played most of our games on well-manicured diamonds with good umpires. The fields, for the most part, were well maintained. The infield was a mixture of dirt and sand, and the outfield was grass. A couple of fields were grass fields surrounded by corn fields. These fields were exceptions to the rule. It was like playing in the movie *Field of Dreams*. We were surrounded by corn that stood at least six to eight feet tall.

Ready for state tournament

Danville Steel's Tomahawks, boasting a 21-1 record, will represent the Danville area in the ASA women's state slow pitch tournament, Friday through July 23, in Decatur. The Tomahawks won the Danville regional crown July 4 at Ridge Farm. Team members are: front left, Gerald Smith, coach, Deloris Cooper, Linda Hall, Evonda Goings, Sharon Winston, Rosemary Hinton, Oscar Williams, coach. Back Wilbur Adkisson, manager, Judy Criss, Phyllis Smith, Janice Rose, Vickie Beasley, Josie Driver, Linda Cooper, Jimmy Scruggs, coach. Absent are Rose Driver, Brenda Morris, Savannah Jefferson, Marvin Brandon, coach, and Janice Blaylock.

PLAYING AGAINST THE UMPIRES AND OFFICIALS

Occasionally, we would have to play nine players against the two umpires. This meant that the umpires would call the game in favor of the other team. During the sixties and early seventies, racism was very prevalent. Most of the umpires were Caucasian. They were not respectful to our team. These officials would always call plays in favor of our opponents. Anything that was close, such as sliding into a base, a pitched ball, or a runner stealing a base was always called in favor of our Caucasian opponents. Sometimes it was a close call, which made it obvious that it was the wrong call.

DISRESPECTFUL SPECTATORS

This was in the late sixties and early seventies, a decade which carried a lot of baggage, things that were out of the players' control. Some of their spectators were intolerably racist and called us derogatory names. On one occasion, one of the spectators did not like the play that was called on the field. I believe she was the grandmother of a player on the rival team. She threatened to take her belt off her skirt and spank one of our teammates for tagging the incoming runner out. Our team had never witnessed adults acting so irresponsibly and racist. The team we were playing against was a good, experienced team. We loved playing with them, and they brought out the best in us. We didn't like the anger and hatred that their spectators brought to the game. Both teams just wanted to play and have fun.

Off the field, the young ladies on both teams were cordial and respectful to each other. We worked together, and some of us later played for the same college teams.

INTEGRATION

Softball teams were not integrated until 1972. Occasionally, you would see an African American girl on a White team or a Caucasian girl on a Black team. In 1972, junior colleges and colleges had more integration than the city leagues.

The Lady Tomahawks integrated in 1972, when the first Caucasian player joined the team. She played part-time with the team. Later, in the 1980s, Yank had several Caucasian players play at the All-Star games and in some of the tournaments. In the early nineties, there were quite a few integrated teams.

There were a few African American teams in the Philly League. One was the UAW-579 Whippets (coached by Jake) and the Laura Lee Fellowship House. However, Laura Lee did not continue with the Philly League, and the Whippets were coached by Jake, who passed away in 1974. Some of the Whippets joined the

Tomahawks, and other members chose not to participate in the Philly League.

To play another Black team, we had to travel to the East Saint Louis area, South Bend, Indiana, Nashville and Union, City, Tennessee.

GETTING STARTED

In the beginning, the Lady Tomahawks encountered several challenges. Age was one of biggest obstacles that hindered our progress. We were incredibly young and inexperienced. We had not developed into the superstars that we would later become. For the most part, the girls played against older and tougher women, giving them loss after loss. Two of the Lady Tomahawks' rivals were the Thomas Excavating team and the Georgetown team, whose players were older, stronger, and more experienced. Those rival teams had windmill pitchers throwing smoke (fast-pitch balls), which was a challenge to the Tomahawks. This made it difficult to play against these two teams. We were no match for what these ladies were throwing.

PITCHING INTIMIDATION

Yank could see that the girls were intimidated by the other teams' pitchers. He told their coaches, "My girls are young, and they are learning the game. They will not stay young and green. They will grow up and learn to play the game." About three years later, we had finally grown into a spectacular superstar team. We finally defeated the top two teams in our league, Thomas Excavating and Georgetown. From that moment on, the Danville Lady Tomahawks never looked back.

DEVELOPMENT OF A YOUNG TEAM

Yank was determined that his young team would not lose because of inadequate pitching. He took his team across town and had a meeting with us. He reassured his young team that they would learn how to hit fast-pitched balls. Yank, along with several young ladies he had trained to pitch, began pitching to the team during practice. Boy, could those ladies throw smoke! Yank himself could really throw a mean fastball with plenty of speed (smoke) sliders. He could also throw change-ups, drop balls, rise balls, and curve balls. Believe me when I say you did not want to be hit by his fast-pitch balls.

Yank knew that Jake had several older girls who could pitch a fastball: a catcher and a few other players. When we went to tournaments, they would travel with us. With the additional players, the Tomahawks became a force to be reckoned with when participating in various tournaments around Illinois and Indiana.

At the same time, his young pitchers and

his young team became more experienced, improving their base running skills, batting, and fielding, and developing their love for the game. We began winning. The Tomahawks were winning games!

THE ADKISSON FAMILY

Wilbur C. Adkisson was known as "Big Yank" or "Yank." Yank was happily married to a successful cosmetologist named Minnie Geneva ("Gen") Johnson-Adkisson. Yank and Geneva both moved to Danville, Illinois from Tennessee.

Yank was born in Kingston Springs, Tennessee and his family moved to Nashville, Tennessee when he was a young man. Geneva was born and raised in Union City, Tennessee. Yank and Geneva met in Nashville where Geneva was pursuing a career in cosmetology at Madelyn Walker's cosmetology school. Yank, at that time, was pursuing a career in the Negro baseball league. He worked at the Washington manufacturing plant. Yank and Geneva fell in love and were united in marriage on January 6, 1949, in Union City, Tennessee. From this union, five beautiful children were born.

Geneva and Yank were well respected in their community. Geneva worked for over fifty years as a professional cosmetologist. She owned her own establishment called Gen's Beauty Shop.

Geneva was a very proud proprietor of her business and held licenses in Tennessee and Illinois. Geneva was exceptionally supportive of her husband's baseball playing, his job, and his Lady Tomahawks softball team.

Mrs. Geneva Adkisson

ARE YOU YOUR BROTHER'S KEEPER?

Yank worked at General Motors during the week, played baseball on the weekends, and managed the Lady Tomahawks after work. He was very involved with his community. Yank was not only an alderman, but he served in his church as well. He was family oriented and a provider. He loved his wife, children, and relatives. He made sure his family was always taken care of. He was definitely a family man.

Yank simultaneously coached the men's UAW 579 softball team during the summer months, and men's UAW 579 basketball team in the winter months.

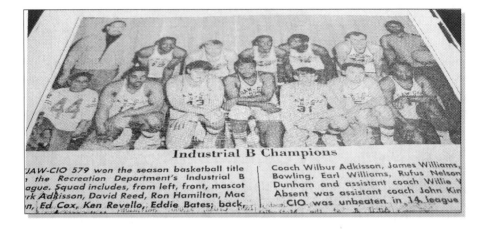

Industrial B Champions

UAW-CIO 579 won the season basketball title the Recreation Department's Industrial B ague. Squad includes, from left, front, mascot rk Adkisson, David Reed, Ron Hamilton, Mac n, Ed Cox, Ken Revello, Eddie Bates; back, Coach Wilbur Adkisson, James Williams, Bowling, Earl Williams, Rufus Nelson Dunham and assistant coach Willie Absent was assistant coach John Ki CIO was unbeaten in 14 league

He followed Danville High School football, basketball, and track teams. He often became the community chauffeur for the young teenagers who needed rides to the high school games in neighboring towns such as Champaign, Decatur, and Bloomington, Illinois. He was his brother's keeper. He would cut his neighbors' grass, shovel snow, give rides to those who didn't have transportation, bring coal to them for their furnaces in the winter, and from time-to-time purchase groceries for those who had fallen into challenging times.

LIFE AFTER THE WAR

PLAYING PROFESSIONAL NEGRO BASEBALL

As a child, Yank loved the game of baseball. He played at a lot of sandlots and pickup games. As he grew into adulthood, World War II was at the forefront. Tennessee was a volunteer state with an army made up of lots of young ambitious young people. Yank was one of the young men who went to war to serve his country and fought for the freedoms we enjoy today.

In the military, Yank became an excellent sharpshooter, played baseball, and was a member of the Engineer Basic Dump Truck Company, mainly made up of African American truck drivers. It was a large convoy of trucks that carried supplies behind the enemy lines. He hauled ammunition, rock, cement, lumber, engineer's equipment, and quartermaster's supplies. He drove 150 miles daily over all types of roads and terrain, and under blackout conditions. He had to service and make repairs to his own truck.

Yank received an honorable discharge from the army. While in the military, he had the honor to meet and play with some of the legends of the game: Joe DiMaggio, Enos Slaughter, Satchel Paige (Leroy Robert), Josh Gibson, Roy Campanella, and the young Jackie Robinson.

One of his favorite childhood friends was James "Zipper" Zapp. James and Yank both grew up in Nashville, Tennessee. Both men served in the United States military.

Mr. Wilbur "Yank" Adkisson

They served in the United States military and traveled the United States chasing their first love: baseball. Yank referred to this as his chitterling circuit of baseball. Both men played, sometimes together and sometimes opposite each other. Yank and James played for the Negro League, while Yank played for the Nashville Club and New Royals. Both teams were farm teams of the Baltimore Elite Giants of the Negro National League. James played for the Nashville Cubs in the Negro League and went on to pursue a career with the Birmingham Black Barons. This put both men on different journeys for their quest to play professional baseball.

Mr. Wilbur "Yank" Adkisson and Mr. James Zapp

OPPORTUNITY ONLY KNOCKS ONCE

Yank's golden opportunity finally arrived. It was a dream come true. He was recruited to try out for the Philadelphia Athletics. It was a major league franchise. This was something he had worked very hard to achieve. Shortly after receiving the call (a telegram), it was very disappointing that he did not get a chance to answer this once in a lifetime call. Yank was playing with the Norfolk Giants when he received that long-awaited telegram. He had just broken his ankle. It was a very unexpected, sad, and upsetting time in his life. Yank did not want to leave his team. It was late in the baseball season, and he was afraid he wouldn't be strong enough to have a good showing. He thought it would be better to wait and go to spring training with his team. Unfortunately, he chose to bypass this call. They never called him again. Opportunity only knocks once. You should always answer the call when given the opportunity.

Because of his injured leg, Yank had to return

to his hometown of Nashville, Tennessee and recuperate. After he had recovered from his leg injury, he decided to relocate to Danville, Illinois for spring training with the Danville Dans. He regrouped and moved to Danville, Illinois in 1952. The Danville Dans were a class D minor league farm team for the Milwaukee Braves. They were part of the Mississippi-Ohio Valley League, also known as MOV. Yank played with the Danville Dans, but it was disappointing that he never received the call to come back and play with the Philadelphia Athletics team. The Philadelphia Athletics team relocated to Kansas City on November 5, 1954.

MOVING ON WITH LIFE

While attending a luncheon for baseball players hosted by the Kiwanis at the Wolford Hotel, Yank found himself sitting across the table from the manager of the local General Motors automotive plant in Danville, Illinois. By the end of lunch, the manager of General Motors had offered Yank a job. He accepted the job offer after the baseball season. Yank was gainfully employed with General Motors for twenty-eight years. He retired in 1980.

While working at GM, he raised a family, and continued playing baseball with the Danville Dans, the GM UAW team, the Laura Lee Fellowship, and the Champaign Eagles. Baseball was his life and he lived for the game.

He wasn't one to sit down and enjoy his retirement. Yank believed a man should work if possible. One of his favorite quotations from the Bible was, "If a man doesn't work, he should not eat" (2 Thessalonians 3:10). Yank later applied to the East Central Illinois Community Action Agency. He was hired and worked in the weatherization department until he had a stroke in 1998.

He loved the outdoors and his community. When Yank could no longer devote his life to playing baseball, he continued working with the Lady Tomahawks softball team.

THE WOMAN WHO STOOD BESIDE THE MAN

Minnie Geneva Adkisson, who stood beside Yank, held a cosmetology license in Tennessee and Illinois. Geneva was very proud of her accomplishments. Gen is the name she preferred to go by. She was also an instructor of cosmetology.

Gen's Beauty Shop

Gen encouraged other African American women to keep abreast of the latest workshops and everything in their occupations. She attended professional workshops and seminars and loved her profession.

Gen was an incredibly supportive wife. She enjoyed watching the Lady Tomahawks play and spending time with them. She was their number one financial contributor and fan. Gen felt that the girls should look their best on and off the field. She did not mind sharing her husband with the community and with the Lady Tomahawks. She felt that the girls needed positive leadership and a safe place to have fun. Gen knew that the girls would find safety with her husband. "The Lady Tomahawks were it!"

INTERESTING FACTS

Yank

Wilbur "Yank" Clinton Adkisson

Born: December 27, 1923

Place: Nashville, Tennessee

Height: 6'1"

United States Army: World War II corporal; received the Bronze Star, Good Conduct Medal, and the Army Service Ribbon

Married: Fifty-one years to Minnie Geneva "Gen" Johnson-Adkisson

Lived: Danville, Illinois

Children: Five

Occupation: Labor inspector for General Motors for twenty-five years

Danville Community Action Weatherization Program in 1997

Sports: Baseball, fast-pitch softball, slow-pitch softball, and basketball

Park: Adkisson Park (Carver Park) in 1999

Founder and Manager: The Danville Lady Tomahawks

Coached: The Danville Lady Tomahawks for forty-three years

Music: The Spinners and Rhythm and Blues

Special Attribute: Left-handed batter (could switch hit if needed)

Position played professionally: Left field

Minnie "Gen" Geneva Jonson-Adkisson

Born: April 7, 1927

Place: Union City, Tennessee

Married: Wilbur "Yank" C. Adkisson, also known as "Big Yank"

Lived: Danville, Illinois

Children: Five

Occupation: Cosmetologist (fifty-two years)

License: Tennessee and Illinois

Clubs: Member of Anderson Street Block Club, Aries and Taurus Club, Allen Chapel Church AME Ladies Auxiliary Board, Bradley-Mayberry American Legion Post #136, and the High School Alumni Club

Hobbies: Loved music, singing, sewing, gardening, and supporting the Danville Lady Tomahawks

Mr. and Mrs. Adkisson

THE TOMAHAWKS ROLL CALL AND THAT LITTLE BROWN BAT

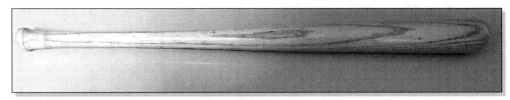

Little Brown Bat

The Tomahawk roll call was done by Yank using a little brown bat. When Yank raised the bat above his head, we knew it was time to take the field (this happened in the earlier years). Yank was disciplined and instilled discipline in his players. He treated his team with respect.

Sports

Danville slow-pitch squad continues its domination

By FRED KRONER
News-Gazette Staff Writer

DANVILLE — Wilbur Adkisson started coaching summer recreation softball teams 31 years ago.

When the Tomahawks debuted as a fast-pitch team in 1964, there was no indication the franchise would survive for decades.

"We lost our first 15 games," Adkisson recalled.

That year, however, was the only one in which the team — now known as the Untouchable Tomahawks — had a losing record.

Since 1976, the Tomahawks have played in slow-pitch leagues. Last season, Adkisson's group placed fourth in the Class A state tournament.

This year's squad is 18-2 while competing in Danville's A League and is preparing for an appearance in the state major league tournament, which starts July 22 in Champaign. Adkisson believes the Tomahawks are prepared for the advanced competition.

"This team is stronger," he said. "It's stronger defensively. It's stronger in hitting. It's stronger in every phase."

Three key off-season additions helped solidify the lineup.

One newcomer is outfielder Felicia Austin, who joined the team last year in time for the state tournament and earned All-State honors. She plays regularly this season and is the team's top home run hitter.

Catcher Danielle Davis and

> Wilbur Adkisson's squad is 18-2 while competing in Danville's A League and is preparing for an appearance in the state major league tourney, which starts July 22 in Champaign. Adkisson believes his team is prepared for the advanced competition.

outfielder Rolana Brown are the other newcomers.

The Tomahawks' other returning All-Staters are shortstop Linda Cooper and outfielder Ann Severado, who has been shifted to second base.

Adkisson said it's "the love of the game," that has prompted him to continue coaching.

The enjoyment and satisfaction have increased, he said.

"It's even better," he said. "As the players get trained, you don't have to work as hard with them."

At one time, Adkisson also coached a feeder team, the Junior Tomahawks. Among the players who have moved up are Cooper, outfielder Evonda Goings, utility player Josie Driver, pitcher Joann Cunningham and left-handed first baseman Yvonne Summers.

Adkisson is starting to see second-generation players wearing the Tomahawks'

uniform, and he likes it.

His third baseman is Melissa Stone, whose mother Shirley "played on the first team I had."

Melissa Stone, he said, "is one of the unsung players who is a solid third baseman."

Summers' daughter is being groomed for the future.

"Kapreia Kirk will be my next shortstop," Adkisson said. "I'm bringing her along slowly and building her confidence."

Kirk, an upcoming sophomore at Danville High School, is one of the area's premier distance runners. She was a state qualifier in cross-country and track as a freshman.

Among the players relied on for power besides Austin and Cooper are Driver and extra hitter Laura Walls. Walls homered Wednesday in a 16-2 conquest of A League runner-up Gatsby.

Cunningham is the pitching ace for a team that has successfully defended its city A League championship.

The team has lost just once since its opener, when 22 runs wasn't enough to secure a victory.

"The flood washed out the diamond at Carver Park," Adkisson said. "We got off to a bad start. We didn't have any place to practice before our first game (a 23-22 loss)."

A final tally showed 21 softball teams in Danville's three women's leagues. The Untouchable Tomahawks will be the city's only representative in the major league state tourney.

BEAUTIFUL MEMORIES BY THE LADY TOMAHAWKS!

JOAN CUNNINGHAM

The Lady Tomahawks were:

- Loyal
- Disciplined
- Faithful
- Committed
- Dedicated

We were on fire!

LINDA COOPER

- Coach Adkisson was a great man and an awesome coach.
- I cherish the moments we had with him and the team. When we get older, it will be nothing but memories.
- We couldn't wait until after Easter for spring training and conditioning.
- Coach Adkisson was dedicated to the upkeep of the softball diamond. It was smooth as butter—the best infield ever.
- The softball/baseball bereavement mitt was designed by Coach Adkisson. This mitt was designed to honor the deceased members of our team. It was shaped like a softball mitt with a beautiful mixture of flowers that was used in a standing spray at team members' funerals.
- He was a father figure.
- Becoming city champions
- Defending our back-to-back titles, year after year
- Team pictures
- Newspaper write-ups about the Tomahawks

Anonymous Team Member

- That little brown bat for Tomahawk roll call
- Yank was wonderful!
- I feel blessed to be a part of what became a household name—*Tomahawks*—in Danville, Illinois.
- Yank gave me some of the best days of my life for so many years.
- The names Yank Adkisson and Tomahawks will live on forever!

SHIRLEY NEWSOME-GLENN

- During my time playing with the Tomahawks, we were truly a family.
- "When one hurts, we all hurt". "We cried together, and we laughed together".
- We were family.
- Mr. and Mrs. Adkisson became our parents.
- Each young lady on the team took care of the younger sisters.
- We grew in strength, wisdom, and knowledge of softball.
- There is no greater love than to have been with all of the ladies all of those years.

Thank you to Ronald, Steve, and Little Mark for holding us up.

CANDICE SMITH—MY GRANDFATHER

- I was so excited when I got to play on his team.
- Not only did I play on his team, I played a game with my mother, one of the original Lady Tomahawks.

Candice Smith batting

KAPREIA SHARIF

- Yank was a great teacher of the game.
- He brought out the best in me and taught me to play the game at a higher level.
- He was a father figure to the team.
- The players became family.
- I would recommend playing softball to young girls.
- One of my best moments was hitting a triple against the number one team.

LINDA HALL

- Love it!
- So proud to be one of the Lady Tomahawks!
- One of the best times of my life
- Yank was an awesome coach.
- The many years I played on this team will always be a special memory in my life.
- Tomahawks forever!

TERRY ENOXIS-MADDOX

Thank you for allowing me the opportunity to expound on my adventures being a member of the dynamic Danville Lady Tomahawks softball team, under the management of Coach Yank Adkisson.

I started my softball journey in the late 1960s at fourteen years of age playing with Coach Jake Butler. I played the catcher position. When Coach Butler passed away, our team dissolved, and I was asked by Coach Yank Adkisson to join the Lady Tomahawks as catcher. The Tomahawks were one of the most revered teams in the league with an awesome winning record. I was so proud to be a member.

The team traveled to different towns in the area as well as some out of state. Union City, Tennessee comes to mind as one of the most memorable events. When we took to the field to play, we noticed that some of the opposing players had no shoes on and no gloves/mitts. We loaned them our gloves/mitts. It was a close game, but the Tomahawks prevailed and won the tournament. It was my first experience traveling out of state. Our coaching staff went above and beyond to make us feel comfortable and safe for the entire weekend of fun in the sun.

Oftentimes, after playing games and before going home, Coach would treat us to Marty K's or other burger joints to show his appreciation, whether we won or lost. At no time had I ever heard Coach negatively criticize, demean, or scold a fellow teammate. That's what made our team winners because Coach Adkisson really cared, and it showed.

PHYLLIS ADKISSON-SMITH

Yank was my father. He is deceased and a part of him is stored in my heart. I would like to share my memories on the memory wall of the Lady Tomahawks.

Playing softball with my sister Tomahawks is an experience I will never forget. It was one of the best times of my life. We became not only one of the greatest teams ever to play this game, but we became sisters under one cause. That cause was to become great students of the game of softball. We were united in sisterhood. For me, there was no experience like it. We made memories and softball history. We became legends in our hometown. We were a household name that I hope will never be forgotten. We learned a lot about the game and a lot about life. My father was not only a coach, but also a teacher of life experiences. He was a father for those who did not have fathers. There is no greater honor on this earth than to invest in children, the future generation. There are no words to explain what he meant to me and to the team. My father was dedicated year after year to the team. He saw a need in the community, and he met that need. He taught discipline and respect as well as respect for the other team.

GREATEST MOMENTS FOR ME (MRS. PHYLLIS ADKISSON-SMITH)

1. My Softball Debut: After sitting on the bench from an early age, I finally got to play at Lincoln Park at the age of twelve. I was so happy! I felt like I had finally broken into the starting line-up, even though it was the last inning of the game. This was so special!
2. Learning to play every position of the game.
3. Learning the rules of the game.
4. Learning how to keep the scorebook.
5. Learning to respect the ladies on our team and on the other team.
6. Respect for the officials as well as the spectators.
7. Loved the fast-pitch game.
8. Becoming a very strong left-handed batter.
9. Hitting homeruns.
10. Being able to walk on any team and make the starting line-up.
11. Traveling and learning about the world as an impressionable young lady.
12. Playing on my college teams.

13. Playing on the Texas traveling team and coming in sixth in the United States (slow-pitch in Houston, Texas).

14. Most Inspiring Moment: The Danville Philly League All-Star Fast Pitch Team (1976 position: short-stop).

15. Most Valuable Player 1978, short stop at the Producer Park Tournament

16. Slow Pitch: Playing softball with my daughter on the Danville Lady Tomahawks in the summer of 1990.

17. The best memory was riding in that pink and black station wagon with my sisters, singing, "Everywhere we go people want to know, who we are, so we tell them, we are the Tomahawks, the mighty, mighty Tomahawks."

THE DANVILLE PHILLY LEAGUE ALL-STAR TEAM

Phyllis Adkisson and other Philly League All-Star Team Members

Phyllis Adkisson, Producers Park
Most Valuable Player in 1978

GREAT-GRANDDAUGHTER'S DEDICATION: CIARA SMITH

My great-grandfather sounds like an incredible man, even though I never had a chance to meet him. All the stories I have heard lead me to believe that he was an inspiration to everyone, male and female.

ROYAL THRILL ARTICLE

Adkisson gets royal thrill
from a certain home run

DANVILLE — He's a man who played baseball in the service with Jackie Robinson, had Buck Leonard hit a ball over his head in right, played left field behind Satchel Paige, and was close enough to hear Josh Gibson 'razz' a teammate.

But when it comes to telling stories, Danville's Wilbur Adkisson likes the one about the home run he hit off of Tom Fletcher at Royal in 1959.

Adkisson and Fletcher, the father of current Montreal All-Star catcher Darrin Fletcher who pitched one game in the majors himself, were teammates on the Twilight League Wolverines, but played against each other in the Eastern Illinois League — Fletcher with Royal, and Adkisson with the all-black Champaign Eagles.

"In the Twilight League, we played out at Garfield Park on Sunday mornings at 11," Adkisson recalled. "It was the end of the season, and we were playing for the championship game of the Twilight League. Our Wolverine team, with Tommy and all the rest, we beat a team out here at Garfield Park for the championship, but Tommy didn't pitch that game. Joe Kroger pitched.

"Then we loaded up the car and we all raced to Royal. We were enemies at that time," he chuckled. "Tommy, Les Bushoom and those guys were playing for Royal, and me and the others would play for the Eagles."

Royal won the game, in a contest Adkisson called a "great battle.

"Royal had the lead, Tommy was pitching," Adkisson said.

See **ADKISSON** Page 3B

Commercial-News photo
by Roy Dabner

Wilbur Adkisson reminisces about his baseball career Wednesday night before coaching a softball game at Douglas Park.

■ Ackisson recalls a few baseball legends /3B

Adkisson
Continued from Page 1B

"Walt Moore came up, it was something like the third or fourth inning. He hit one into right center that stuck into the top of the fence," Adkisson said. "Our manager, Wardell Jackson, argued that it should be a home run, but the umpire gave us two bases. Then at this point, Jackson looks at the ump and says, 'All right 'ump, you called that double? Let's see what you're going to call the next one.'

"That kind of motivated me, because I knew he had a whole lot riding on what I could do," Adkisson said. "I came to bat, and Les Bushoom was catching. He caught for us out here, too. He called me 'Ak' all the time. He said, 'Ak, wouldn't you rather be playing with Tommy than against him?'

"I said, 'No, I love to hit against left-handers.' So he says, 'All right Tommy, he loves you, he loves to hit against you. Let's give him this one.'

"I figured right then, he was going to throw his curve ball," he said. "With me playing center field behind him all the time, I knew how his curve ball would break. He had a little hitch in his move. When he would get ready to throw, he would kind of jerk, and I knew what was coming when I saw him kick that leg up."

At the same time, Adkisson said he could hear a voice from along the first-base line. A very familiar voice.

"Andy Cohen was pulling for Tommy, you know," Adkisson said. "I could hear him over there talking. If you ever hear him talk, you'll know what I mean.

"Stick it in his ear, Tommy! Stick it in his ear!"

"Andy will deny that today, but I could hear that voice," Adkisson laughed. "He's the only one that has a voice that sounds like that.

"So, when Tommy wound up like that, I knew what was coming, and I dug in on him," Adkisson said. "Here come that old curve, and I hit it a mile over that right-field fence. We went ahead 3-2, and went on to beat them 5-2."

Adkisson, who grew up in Nashville, Tenn., came to Danville in 1952 when he joined the Class D Danville Dans of the Boston Braves organization in the Missouri-Ohio Valley or M-O-V League.

He had served in the armed forces during World War II, and played several years in the Negro Leagues for the Nashville Cubs and Norfolk-Newport News Royals, both farm teams of the Baltimore Elite Giants of the Negro National League.

He played with the Dans in 1952, earning $275 per month. It wasn't enough to raise a family on, however.

"The money wasn't there, and when I had the opportunity to earn more money working for General Motors, that's where I went," Adkisson said. "I worked for General Motors, settled down here in Danville, and started my family life."

Adkisson married his wife, Geneva, in 1951.

"There was no point in me trying to play ball," he said. "It wasn't paying off. I had to make a decision and I'm proud that I made that decision."

Adkisson hurt his back when he stepped into soft ground while lifting a picnic table in 1958, ending his career with the Eagles. But he continued playing ball for a few years, and began coaching the Tomahawks women's softball team in 1964.

He's still with the Tomahawks. Last year the team finished fourth in the state. Adkisson said he hopes to return next year for the 31st year with the club.

GROUP WANTS TO RENAME PARK

Group wants to rename park

■ NAACP backing Adkisson to honor as mentor, coach

By NOELLE McGEE
News-Gazette Staff Writer

DANVILLE — For more than 30 years, Wilbur Adkisson taught young women to play softball at Carver Park.

Now a local group wants the park to bear his name.

"Here's a guy who was a professional baseball player with the Negro Leagues and went on to make a great contribution to the community through his leadership, guidance and mentoring," said David Groves, president of the local chapter of the NAACP.

"Normally, we honor and rec-ognize folks once they're deceased," continued Groves, who on Tuesday asked city officials to consider renaming the small park on East Williams Street in Adkisson's honor. "I think we should show our respect and gratitude for all he's done while he's still alive."

City officials believe the park and the public housing complex across the street, which was turn down a few years ago, were named for George Washington Carver, the black educator and inventor. Mayor Bob Jones said staffers are looking into whether the park can be renamed. If it can't, such as in a case where the land was donated, he would suggest naming the baseball diamond where Adkisson spent countless evenings for him instead.

"I certainly think that would be an appropriate thing to do," he said, adding the city council would have the final say.

One alderman said if the park can be renamed, he doesn't know of anyone more deserving than Adkisson, who was a colleague at the East Central Community Action Agency and has been his next-door neighbor for 18 years.

"He gave so much to that park," Lea Brown recalled. "He coached a women's softball team there for probably more than 30 years. He probably taught most of the African-American women in this town how to play softball ... And he was always down there dragging the field, lining it and mak

See PARK, A-10

The Danville chapter of the NAACP wants to rename Carver in honor of Wilbur Adkisson, a longtime softball coach.

BIG YANK'S SAYINGS

1. "When you are off the field, dress like a lady and carry yourself as a lady. Always look your best."
2. Sometimes in practice or during a game, when a hard-hit ball would hit a player on the arm or leg and she didn't react in time to catch it, Yank would joke, "Beat her up, ball."
3. If a base runner was running too slowly around the bases in a game, he would say, "Unhitch your trailer."
4. "Don't trash talk the other team. Let your bat and glove do your talking."
5. "We play to win!"
6. "You are only as good as your weakest player."
7. "Everyone should be able to play every position."
8. "If a man will not work, he shall not eat" (2 Thessalonians 3:10 KJV)
9. "When you are on the softball field, play like a man, and when you are off the field, always dress and carry yourself like a young lady."

THE LADY TOMAHAWK GAME SONG

Everywhere we go
People want to know
Who we are
So, we tell them
We are the Tomahawks
The mighty, mighty Tomahawks!

Repeat
Conclusion
The Tomahawks yeah!

HOME FIELD

George Carver Park was renamed
Adkisson Field in 2000.

Adkisson Park Sign

DANVILLE CITY PARKS PLAYED IN

Adkisson (formerly Carver) Park
Douglas Park
Ellsworth Park
Lincoln Park
Meade Park

UNIFORM COLORS

*1960: White base trimmed in red and blue (tops and bottoms; bottoms were shorts)

*1970: Navy blue tops and bottoms (shorts) trimmed in white

*1980: Tops were gold and navy; bottoms were navy blue shorts

*1990–2000: Tops were navy blue and pants were long gray baseball pants

1960: A few of the original
Tomahawks after a game.
Original uniforms: red, white, and blue

THREE ORIGINAL TOMAHAWKS

Tomahawks Jerseys

PLACES PLAYED
(NOT ALL LISTED)

Midwest/Illinois
Champaign
Danville
Decatur
East St. Louis
Georgetown
Hoopeston
Rankin
Ridge Farm
Indiana
Decatur
South Bend
Terre Haute
Tennessee
Nashville
Union City

PLAYED UNDER OTHER SPONSORS

Tomahawks/Untouchables—The
Danville Motorcycle Club
Tomahawks—UAW 579
Marvis Iron and Metal (Marvis Steel)

Local Sponsors

Gen's Beauty Shop
Dr. Fred Crockett
Dr. William Henderson
Anna Dees McCoy's Barbershop
Motorcycle Club Untouchable
Modest Gas Station
Priscilla's Restaurant
Savannah's Hair Salon
Hoosiers Barbecue
Kag's Barbecue

My apologies to those who aren't listed.

Thank you so much for your kind
generosity and support throughout
the years. You are appreciated.

RIVAL TEAMS IN THE DANVILLE PHILLY LEAGUE

SOME TEAMS THE TOMAHAWKS PLAYED AGAINST IN THE DANVILLE PHILLY LEAGUE (CITY LEAGUE)

Fast-Pitch

Thomas Excavating

Blacks Hardware

Georgetown

General Electric

Westville

Lincoln Park UAW 579

Quaker Oats

Peterson

Slow-Pitch

Paper Dolls

Carmack

Thrifty Muffler

Ridgeway

Franks

Shooting Stars

Laura Lee

Weiss

CERTIFICATE
AMATEUR SOFTBALL
ASSOCIATION

MEN_____   FP_____   YOUTH_____   STATE REGIONAL FINISH _1ST_____

WOMEN _X____   SP _X____   DIVISION _A____   STATE REGIONAL PLAYED IN _DANVILLE_
                            (AA-A-B etc.)

Amateur Softball Association
of America

TEAM MEMBER
THIS IS TO CERTIFY THAT

TOMAHAWKS

located at _DANVILLE, IL_

having duly qualified in accordance with the laws of the Association is entitled to all the benefits and privileges of MEMBERSHIP in the

AMATEUR SOFTBALL ASSOCIATION OF AMERICA

for the year ending _Dec. 31_ 19 _96_

AMATEUR SOFTBALL
ASSOCIATION
OF AMERICA

Carol Frank
COMMISSIONER

For _Danville_

TOMAHAWKS TEAM CAPTAINS

1960 Fast-Pitch: Cassandra Lillard-Reed

1960 Fast-Pitch: Shirley Newsome-Glenn

Fast-Pitch and Slow-Pitch: Judy Criss (Lillard)

1970 Fast-Pitch and Slow-Pitch:
Phyllis Adkisson-Smith (Producer Park
Tournament Most Valuable Player 1976)

1970 Slow-Pitch: Delores Cooper-Forrest

1970 Fast-Pitch and Slow Pitch: Judy Criss
(Lillard) and Phyllis Adkisson-Smith

1980 Slow-Pitch: Linda Cooper (All-Star
Team and Most Valuable Player in 1990)

1980 Slow-Pitch: Linda Cooper
and Evonda Goings

1980 Slow-Pitch: Joan Cunningham

THE TOMAHAWKS BAT BOY(S) AND BAT GIRL(S)

Steve Adkisson*

Mark Adkisson*

Eric Lillard

Kapreia Kirk-Sharif

*Sons of Mr. Adkisson

Sincere apologies if your name is not listed.

Thank you; your work is appreciated.

Special thank you to the boys and men who helped with the upkeep of the Carver Park Softball Field

TOMAHAWKS COACHING STAFF

Wilbur "Yank" Adkisson, Founder,
Manager, and Head Coach
Ronald Adkisson*
Vertie Taylor
Willie Lee Williams
Marvin Brandon
Edgar Driver
Junior Ray Taylor
Junior Ray Duckworth
Elmore "Mo" Battle
Oscar Williams
Jimmy Scruggs
Gerald Smith
Juan Moore
*Son

HONORABLE MENTION

Mr. Nate "BoBo" Smalls, former member of the Indianapolis Clowns baseball team, who occasionally assisted Yank in softball practice.

Mr. Nathaniel Small

ALL-STAR
SOFTBALL TEAM

Picking all-star softball team half the battle

By FRED KRONER
News-Gazette Staff Writer

DANVILLE — Cuba Poulson feels a little uneasy being chosen as one of the two all-stars on Carmack's women's softball team.

As the pitcher on a 23-1 team which won the regular-season title in the competitive Douglas Park League, Poulson realized she had glowing credentials.

"I feel our team is a team of all-stars," said the Catlin resident. "I think it's hard to choose.

"I hate the idea that the whole team

■ Rosters in Scoreboard, B-4.

can't play."

When the inaugural East Central Illinois all-star doubleheader starts at 6:30 p.m. Friday at Douglas Park, Poulson and outfielder Cindy Myers will be the Carmack representatives on the 20-player squad which encompasses the 13-team league.

The Douglas League standouts will take on their counterparts from the Ellsworth Park League.

Poulson, who has pitched most of

the 16 years she's played softball, felt more at home on the mound this summer. She credits the move of the mound from 46 feet to 50 feet from home plate as the reason she's more at ease.

"It's much safer," she said. "I'd gotten to the point I was afraid of the ball. I've gotten cracked in the kneecaps too many times.

"I had played second base because of the shyness. Now I have more time to react. I feel a lot more comfortable."

Among Poulson's teammates Friday will be two stars of the Tomahawk

team, which Carmack faced in Tuesday's city tournament championship game.

Tomahawk, 26-4 for the summer, scored a 5-2 win Tuesday. Shortstop Linda Cooper, who hit .702 in league play, was 3 for 4 and outfielder Lisa Dye was 2 for 4.

Cooper started playing with the Tomahawks before she was a teenager and is now completing her 10th season in the league. She has been regarded as the premier women's

See SOFTBALL, B-4

DECEASED
TOMAHAWKS

Cassandra Lilliard-Reed
Evonda Goings
*Lavern Smith-Brown
*Yvonne Smith-Tyson
Janice Blaylock
Armenna Red- Brown
Mae Olla Duckworth
Shelly Foster-Lillard
Claretha Davis-Adkins
Sue Young
Willa Mae Bankhead
Martha Wright
*Twin sisters

DECEASED TOMAHAWKS COACHES

Mr. Yank Adkisson
Mr. Ronald Adkisson
Mr. Elmore "Mo" Battle
Mr. Edgar Driver ("Nine")
Mr. Vertie Taylor
Mr. Willie Lee Williams

SPECIAL RECOGNITION

Mr. Jake Butler, founder and manager of UAW 579 Whippets

Played in Danville Parks and Recreational League AAU

Home Park: Lincoln Park

Location: Danville, Illinois

Team Nickname: The Whippets

FACTS

The Tomahawks were a force to be reckoned with. Their hard work and determination paid off game after game. They were known throughout the great state of Illinois and its neighboring states. Their name became a household name. Young girls dreamed about being a part of the team and they could not wait to turn twelve so that they could play. May the Tomahawk name live on in the hearts and minds of the citizens of Danville, Illinois. May God bless every young lady, the coaches, and the spectators who supported the Danville Lady Tomahawks.

Phyllis and Yank (father) Adkisson

Mr. Adkisson's great-granddaughter (C. Smith)

DEDICATION

This book is dedicated to the loving memory of my parents, Wilbur and Geneva Adkisson.

My parents were a strong pillar in the African American community. They provided a safe place for young ladies through the Danville Tomahawk softball program.

To all my family and friends, thank you for your support.

A sincere thank you to all the wonderful women who contributed to the Memory Wall.

To God be the Glory

Mrs. Phyllis Adkisson-Smith

Printed in the United States
by Baker & Taylor Publisher Services